Illumination Through Darkness

Poetry That Pours from the Soul

AI Image Notice

Certain images included in this book were created with the assistance of artificial intelligence (AI) tools. All written content, creative vision, and final image selection remain the original work and intellectual property of Ebony Brinson.

Planted in Faith, Rooted in God

The rose doesn't question its thorns, and neither should you. You are the most beautiful thing you will ever create. Your scars, your pain, your growth; every piece of your journey is part of the masterpiece that is you. Be proud of your progress, even when the world only sees thorns.

Grow where you're planted, even in the dirt. What feels unpleasant now is feeding your greatness. Dig deep before you rise; a strong, rooted foundation is essential. Silence isn't punishment; it's preparation. When you finally rise, let your fruit nourish others. Your journey isn't just about you; it's about **leaving something beautiful for the world.**

Table of Contents

BOOK ONE: BROKENNESS

Walk Through Darkness

I walked through shadows, heavy and deep,
Crippled by sickness, robbing me of sleep.
Each step a struggle, every breath a plea.
A body bound, but my spirit fought free.

Betrayal whispered like a trusted friend,
Manipulation spun webs without end.
Deception dressed in comforting lies
left me drowning in tears and silent goodbyes.

Defeated, I wandered, my heart bruised and bare,
A love once cherished dissolved in thin air.
Promises broken, a future erased.
I stood at the edge of love's bitter taste.

But in the wreckage, I found a new voice.
Setting boundaries became my choice.
I let go of the hands that dragged me down,
and wore self-love like a radiant crown.

No longer searching for others to see
that I am enough, I am valid in me.
The darkness taught me what light cannot show.
In losing myself, I learned to grow.

Through sickness, through sorrow,
through love's last sight,
I found the strength to rise and fly.
For in the shadows, I made my stand.
I found myself whole with my heart in my hands.

Painful Truth

I pushed, I shoved, and shattered our love.
A love once whole, now riddled with blame.
You turned away, your silence a blade,
to torture my heart in the void you've made.

Searching for love, for worth, for an embrace,
Yet the mirror reflected the loneliest space.
I sought in others what I failed to see,
That love and acceptance must first start with me.

You run, you hide, behind masks you've designed.
Ego and pride as your fortress confined.
Who are you, truly? Which face is the truth?
So many shadows obscure your youth.

But one face emerges, bitter and stark.
The face of defeat, of lies in the dark.
Lies to yourself, lies to me,
unspoken whispers of a guilty plea.

You turned your back, and I turned mine, too
Finally grasping what's painfully true:
There was, is, and will never be a "me and you."

Once, our love bloomed in vibrant hues,
Petals soft with morning's dewy clues.
We flourished beneath the sun's warm glow,
But now, it's gone- nothing left to show.

Like roses, once rich, fragrant, and bright.
Our love wilted slowly, lost to the night.
Thorns now linger where blossoms had grown,
 leaving us grasping what we've outgrown.
Seasons have passed, and petals lay bare,
Whispers of passion are now lost in the air.
No rain can revive what's already dead.
No sunlight can spark what's withdrawn.

Our love, like a withered rose, lies still,
A bloom that fate will never refill.
What once was beauty, pure and alive,
Now fades in silence, unable to thrive.

So, we let it fall petals to the ground,
A love that is lost, no longer bound.
For some roses bloom, while others burn under the sun.
A love tarnished, lost, never to be found.

Torn Heart

Twisted and distorted
Mutilated and dismantled
Corrupt and destroyed
Lies and deceit
Deception and defeat

All the things you've done to me.
You've ripped my heart from my chest.
You stomped on it, brought me down to my knees.
You kicked and spat on me.
I surrendered to you, submitted to you,
Only to be neglected, rejected, abandoned,
and betrayed by you.

To be used, to be hurt, to be brought
to total shame by you.
Regret, resentment, and guilt are mere thoughts.
How'd we get this way?
When did we fall in so many separate ways?

Through The Struggle

Nobody knows, nobody cares.
Life moves on, through joys and despair.
Whether I stay or whether I go,
time marches on, relentless in flow.

Unseen, unvalued, a shadow untold.
A heart left to freeze, turning bitterly cold.
Why am I screaming in silence so loud?
Yet lost in the noise of an uncaring crowd.

No one listens; no one shares.
Burdened by choices, trapped in my snares.
But perhaps it's not theirs to understand.
This weight is mine to take in hand.

For through the struggle, I'll rise above.
Turning my pain into strength and love.
Though silence surrounds, my spirit will roar,
gaining the upper hand, forevermore.

Abandoned, rejected, a soul left bruised,
manipulated, degraded, and cruelly used.
How much torment can one consume,
Before the heart seeks solace and solitude?

Isolated, drowning in a sea of despair.
Loneliness whispers, no comfort there.
My inner child weeps, lost in the void,
asking why her innocence was destroyed.

Why did you scream? Why did you fight?
Why leave me alone through countless nights?
Now grown, matured, yet still I yearn,
For answers, for healing, for peace to return.

Through shadows I seek the light of resolve,
A broken spirit longing to evolve. Though the past
may echo, hauntingly clear, I'll find my strength
breaking chains of fear.

A Touch

Heavy, my heart, is heavy.
Yearning, my soul, is yearning.
For something new, untouched, untold, for truth.
A touch unspoken, yet deeply aligned.
Undefined, divine, and gently refined.
A grace that lingers, soft and rare.
A love that answers every prayer.

Soul tie Undone

I missed your touch, I missed your feel,
But all we shared was carnal appeal.
A fleeting thrill, our bodies entwined, bound
by lust, not hearts aligned.

You loved me good, yet drained me dry.
You took my light, left me asking why.
I poured my all, uplifted your name, only to
watch you walk away in shame.

It was never love, just a reckless chase.
Sinful desires wrapped in a warm embrace.
I wove dreams from threads of lies.
Blind to the truth that time never denies.

Now the veil is lifted, the truth revealed.
The wounds you left have begun to heal.
Our soul tie broken, the chains undone,
I'm free of the vagabond; I've finally won.

All I Wanted

All I wanted was you.
I begged and pleaded for you.
I changed my ways to please you.
I gave you my body to satisfy you.
I gave you my love. I surrendered to you.
I wanted everything: a life with you.
Now I realize we walk two different paths.

I found myself and lost you, no longer begging
and pleading to be seen by you.
Begging to hear a word from you.
Silence spoke volumes.
Your love hid in places I never knew.
Your love is blind, and I can't read your mind.
I was just someone there to help kill time.
To fill the spaces that could never be filled by my time.

I lost you, and I found me.
I love you, but I love me more.
Putting you before myself, I lost my wealth.
I lost my life, I lost my sanity,
I lost my health. And still, you would never put me first.

Slowly building what you tore away.
Loving myself more and more each day.
Looking in the mirror and realizing self.
I'm beautiful, something you never said.
Saying I love you felt forced,
like being force-fed in a hospital bed.

I once lay in bed and cried thinking of you,
now I sleep at peace knowing I tried with you.
The hurt and pain you've caused set me free in ways
you wouldn't believe.
Thank you for letting me rediscover me.
No longer bound, I'm Set Free!

Let Go

I am transformed. My mind is renewed.
I walk with confidence; I walk in faith.
I am fully restored, fully rejuvenated.
Brought back to life, I've been fully resuscitated.

No longer bound to slavery
No longer bound to sexual immorality
No longer bound to my fear,
no longer bound to my guilt.

Letting go of my past rejection once left me hindered,
traumatized, broken, and abused.
Not just mentally, I've been physically used.
I let go of you. My addiction, my idol.
You who left me abandoned, and full of grief.

Finally letting go, I've found a sense of relief.
I am pure walking in my purpose.
Breaking chains of depression.
Breaking chains of torture.
Breaking chains of the demonic strongholds
created in me.

Breaking the strongholds created
by those before me.
I have the power to do all things,
I constantly remind.
I COMMAND THESE CHAINS ARE BROKEN
In Jesus name.

Losing You

I never knew losing you would be a breakthrough.
When I lost you, I found myself, I found truth.
Once traumatized by your wickedness.
Crippled by your silent antics and deception.

All I wanted was you.
Your heart and your time.
I wanted what was never mine.
So, I let go of what wasted my time.
I found out my heart was all I needed.
I'm a star you tried to pluck out of the sky.

My light, you tried to hide.
Everything that is in the dark must come to light.
I am the light you couldn't find.
The light that left you blind.
But the light that gave you warmth through the storm.
Oh! How that light is gone!
I love the fact that I've accepted Letting Go!

BOOK TWO:
FINDING HIM

Saved From Sin

My soul was filled with darkness,
my heart was corrupt with sin.
My mind was filled with negativity,
no sight of an end.

The trauma, the pain, neglect, and rejection
left a permanent scar on my heart.
These knives have penetrated and pierced
me deep from the start.
Crippling and damaging doubts of self,
leading to expectations of man.

Looking to fill a void no man could ever fill.
The constant repetition of emotional distress.
Disaster, disappointment, doubt,
and torment were my end.

There is nothing left to do but shout out Why?
Weapons formed against self from false
imaginations and curse words spoken.
Questioning who will love this damaged soul?
I'm broken. Wasn't I meant to be loved?

Reliable and dependable, but jealous.
Wasn't I meant to be cherished?
Then I found a friend better than
any man or woman has ever been.

A protector, a provider
A good listener and faithful to the end.
He showered me with unconditional love.
He corrected me when wronged.

Saved By Grace

Today, my dream came true: you died.
Your soul left your body and returned by grace.
God's grace gave you another shot
at this thing called life.
You will live, sayeth the Lord, get up and walk a new life.

The Presence of God

Lying in the breeze of the cool summer heat,
feeling your perfect presence surround me.
You're my King, my first love.
You're the Mighty One above,
I still can't believe you chose me.

Your love and grace entered this space.
You saved me from myself,
my foolish, immature ways.
You saved me from my fears.
You saved me and healed all my pain.
You saved me from my guilt and shame.

No longer dismayed.
Lord, I feel your presence in this place.
Filling our hearts, Filling our minds.
Giving us hope time after time.

Giving us peace and freeing our minds.
You walk before and beside us.
You're forever around us. You are omnipresent.
Your presence and peace will forever surround me.

Guided Path

I've dreamed of you in shadows deep,
I've seen you fall in restless sleep.
I pray a light will pierce the night,
to guide your path, to make it right.

Though you wound me, I still will praise.
Though you harm me, my hands I still raise.
For Jesus saved me, broke my chains.
And through His love, I'll bear this pain.

If He forgives my every sin,
then I can learn to forgive again.
For the lies you sold, the time you stole,
The games you played scarred my soul.

You used my body, dismissed my cries,
 neglected my heart, and fed me lies.
I was never enough in your narrow sight,
Not short enough, not pretty enough,
skin not light enough.

But I'm strong enough to leave you behind.
After wasting years, I've reclaimed my mind.
My heart, my peace, my soul's design,
My sanity and freedom are finally mine.

A Little Prayer

Lord…. You are my Savior.
The Most High God.
I cannot run, nor can I hide
from your presence. You are my God.

You are my Father, my Abba.
You are Jehovah Jireh, my provider.
You make ways out of no way.
You are Jehovah Rapha, my healer.
You've healed me from sickness, all of it undone.

You are Jehovah Shalom, my peace,
The Prince of Peace
that quiets every storm.
I surrender all my ways to walk according to
your grace.

There is none like you. The Most High God.
Lord, I want to praise you.
I lift my voice in praise to please your Holy name.
I remain in you, you remain in me,
we'll be together for eternity.

I Won't Fail

Abandoned, rejected, a soul left bruised,
manipulated, degraded, and cruelly used.
How much torment can one consume
before the heart seeks solace and solitude?

Isolated, drowning in a sea of despair,
Loneliness whispers, no comfort there.
My inner child weeps, lost in the void,
asking why her innocence was destroyed.
Why did you scream? Why did you fight?

Why leave me alone through countless nights?
Now grown, matured, yet still, I yearn.
Yearn for answers, for healing,
for peace to return.

Through shadows, I seek the light of resolve.
A broken spirit longing to evolve.
Though the past may echo, hauntingly clear,
I'll find my strength, breaking chains of fear.
I won't fall; I won't fail!

Saved from Sin

My soul was filled with darkness.
My heart was corrupted with sin.
My mind was filled with negativity,
no sight of an end.

The trauma, the pain, the neglect,
and rejection left a permanent
scar on my heart.
These knives have penetrated and pierced
me deeply from the start.
Crippling and damaging doubts
about self led to expectations of a man.

Looking to fill a void,
I believe no man could ever fill.
The constant repetition of emotional distress.
Disaster, disappointment, and doubt.
Torment was my end, so I thought.

But then I lost you!
At the time, my heart shouted out Why?
Weapons formed against self from false imaginations
and curse words spoken.
Questioning who will love this damaged soul. I'm broken!

Wasn't I meant to be loved?
Reliable and dependable, but I was jealous.
Wasn't I meant to be cherished?
Then, I found a friend better than any man,
or woman has ever been.
A protector, a provider.
A good listener and faithful to the end.

He showered me with unconditional love.
He corrected me when I was wrong.
He keeps me focused. He keeps me strong.
No longer distracted by things of this world.
He's compassionate and worthy of all my love.

Sometimes, I question why he's so good to me.
Why does he constantly choose me?
Why is He so patient with me?
Why does he continue to call me?
Bless me? Why do I feel like I'm not?
Not good enough? Though I died
to live a life with Him.
The desires of my own eyes weakened my flesh.

Pluck them out, so I may sin not.
No longer dragged away into the darkness.
Temptation was birthing a world of sin.
Trembling in fear of my salvation.
Now, fearful and isolated.

Who will love an overthinker full of control?
Who will love this damaged, broken, shattered,
and shadowed girl? Someone who pulled me out
of the slimiest, dirtiest, darkest mud of sin.
He freed me of the addiction to alcohol,
the poison that altered my mind and heart within.

Addiction to fortification and lust.
That caused dark, demonic soul ties.
Unwanted guests are the monitoring foes.
We gladly welcome them in.
The addiction to pill popping,
I almost died. God surely saved my life this time.

Showing me grace, showing me love,
from up above. Can you imagine?
He placed my feet on solid ground.
He told me you are mine.

I will always say yes.
Yes, to the Man who saved my life.
His name is Jesus Christ.
He told me I am more than a conqueror.
Nothing can separate me from his love.

He told me I am fearfully and wonderfully made!
He told me, He will never leave nor me.
I am spirit-made. He asked me, child,
with little faith, Why do you doubt me? Who am I?
That's when I replied: You are my Lord Savior.

The Most High, The Great I am That I am.
The Risen Messiah, The Fourth Man in the fire.
You set my feet on solid ground.
I know you won't ever let me down.
Lord, I love you, Lord, I thank you.
Lord, I trust you, and Lord, I belong to you.
You and You alone.

Can We?

Can we grow old together?
Walk through the storm together.
Strengthen our bond together, can we?
Can we stay strong together?
Learn to forgive each other.
Learn how to love each other, can we?

Can we trust in God to mend our hearts
from the damage that we've caused.
Can we make it right in Jesus Christ
to show us how to love?
Can we learn to trust again?
Can we learn to correct in love?

Uplift and not offend.
Stand our ground together till the end.
Fighting through the crowd together.
Can we fight the good fight together?
Pray through the storm together?
Can we?

Lord, you go before us in all our ways.
Lord, you are our healer, our true redeemer
through the day. Lord, you are King.
The lamp beneath my feet,
lighting the way through the darkness so I may see.
Though I may stumble, I will never fall.

Can we praise together?

Can we shine together?

Can we walk in righteousness and love together?

Can we?

Note To Future Relationship: Amos 3:3
Can two people walk together without agreeing?

Becoming Me

I've wandered through shadows, lost and unsure.
Chasing reflections that couldn't endure.
But in the quiet, I began to see the journey
was less about them but more about me.

I'm learning to listen, to know my own voice.
I discovered in myself a reason to rejoice.
No longer defined by the past, I've outgrown it.
I embrace who I was, but now I love who I am.

With each step, I let God lead the way.
He goes before me, come what may.
When anxious thoughts try to steal my peace,
His presence calms, and fears are released.

When fear draws near, He is my refuge,
strong is His Spirit, I know where I belong.
Made new by grace, washed in His blood,
I rise from the ashes, free by His love.

The darkness that chased me is no longer close.
I've shed old skins and released every fear.
I'm not who I was; that story is done.
A new life has risen, and a new day has begun.

Now, I walk in love, secure and whole,
God's peace, a river flowing through my soul.
With each step forward, I truly believe.
I've found myself, and in Him, I breathe.

The Strength of A Mother

A struggling mother, weary and worn,
Bearing burdens since the day she was born.
A black woman whose voice fights to be heard,
A heart heavy with battles no one can see.

She holds it together by God's mighty grace,
though pain and doubt show on her face.
The weight of the world pulls her down low,
But something unseen won't let her let go.

On nights when she thought of ending it all.
She walks through the storm, steady and strong.
Clinging to faith that carries her along.
Her children, her joy, her reason to fight.

The spark in her soul, the stars in her night.
With every trial, her strength only grows.
She'll protect them both, come what may,
shield them from fear, keep danger at bay.

Her arms are a fortress, her heart a safe place,
A dependable mother with unyielding faith.
I'll always be here," she whispers, sincere.

A reliable mother who wipes every tear.
Through struggles and sorrow,
her love shines bright, a mother who fights
with all her might.

She's more than her burdens, more than her scars.
A woman of courage who reaches for the stars.
And though life's storms may rage and swell.
By God's grace, she knows she will be well.

I Will Not

I will not be stressed, I will not break down.
I refuse to carry the burdens you make.
I won't shoulder the weight that isn't mine.
I've let it go, left it behind.

Yes, I feel lighter, though it stings inside,
admitting the hurt I once tried to hide.
But healing demands I stand my ground.
And peace is the only thing I've found.
I don't want to see you, don't want you near,

The sight of you stirs up all I once feared.
A waste of time, oh, it's clear,
But I've learned to release what won't stay here.
I hold no bitterness, only relief.

Freed from the chains that once brought grief.
What doesn't hold on, I've let it drift away.
And I walk forward lighter each day.

Don't Go Back to Egypt

Don't go back to Egypt, where chains held tight.
where darkness thrived and stole my light.
Don't return to the place that felt like home,
but left me bound, afraid, and alone.

Held in bondage, held in captivity,

A prisoner to your spell, lost in misery.

Sick of the torment that twisted my mind.

I broke free, yet somehow fell back in time.

I taught you much, gave all I could give,

But what did you teach me about how to live?

You taught me to let go, to release the pain.

To run from the lies, not circle in pride.

You showed me the power of trusting God.

I'm not leaning on a man for what I need.

I've learned to trust God, my faithful guide,

the one who lifts me up when cast aside.

He never misleads, never steers me wrong.
He gives me strength and makes me strong.
When you let me down, He carried me through.
Mended my soul and made me new.

So, I won't return to the place I outgrew,
To the hurt, the lies, or the weight of you.
I walk in freedom, whole and restored.
Following the path God has paved
for me to explore. No more Egypt, no chains,
no strife, I choose God's love. I choose my life.

Illumination Through Darkness

I walked in shadows, consumed by fear. Trembling
inside, with darkness near.
Each thought a storm, each breath a weight, whispers
of sickness sealing my fate.

Negativity swirled, thick in the air.
A silent curse from a heart in despair.
If not with my mouth, then with my mind,
I was lost in a lair, cold, dark, and confined.

Anxious, fearful, and bound by stress,
oppressed by burdens, I couldn't confess.
But in that darkness, a spark appeared,
A light that grew a love that cleared.

From the shadows, I began to rise,
healing bright in God's steady eyes.
He lifted the weight and cured my soul.
Like sunlight breaking after endless rain.
My heart is now light, my spirit set free.

 Love took root, replacing misery.
For the light is God, and God is love.
A gift from below and above. In His presence,
I've learned to live, to love others as I love myself.

To forgive and give.

The darkness is gone, and I walk in a new day.

With God beside me, all around me,

walking before me, lighting the path of righteousness.

Access Denied

Access denied to the demons that lurk,
to shadows that gather, to chaos at work.
Access denied to the dark at my side, to fear
that once held me tight.
Access denied to anxiety's tide.

We are free by the blood of Christ.
Set apart, not of this world.
His love, our shield, His light, our heart.
Renouncing the darkness, rejecting its claim,
breaking the bonds in Jesus' name.

For the enemy's armies, their power untrue,
shattered and scattered by grace breaking through. More
than conquerors, we rise and stand.
In Christ, the King, upheld by His hand.

"Cast all your worries," He speaks so near,
"For I am with you; in Me, there's no fear."
1 Peter 5:7, a promise to keep,
In His endless love, our souls find peace.

Found & Made Whole

I was lost, but now I'm found,
Once shattered and chained, now unbound.
Mended by grace, made whole again,
with the Spirit alive, dwelling within.

I call on Jesus. The fire ignites.
A blaze of power, burning inside.
Demons tremble, they scatter and flee.
For I stand in faith, armored with the shield of faith.

The armor of God I wear each day.
In righteousness, I walk His ways.
No weapon formed shall take me down,
In Christ alone, I wear my crown.

Undefeated in Him, He clears my path,
Breaking every curse, destroying every shaky path.
Darkness flees at His mighty name.
Every evil force is put to shame.
I rebuke the devil, and he must flee,

For the Word of God says it, so it shall be.
I crush the serpent beneath my feet,
Victorious in Christ forever, I will be.
No fear, no foe, no chains hold me.

For in Him, I've found true liberty.
Restored, redeemed, I now proclaim:
Jesus reigns, forever the same!

I Trust You

I trust in You, the One who saves.
The One who lights and paves my way.
Through raging storms, I hold You close.
For you've been with me more than most.
Even when it feels as if you're not near,
I feel Your whisper, soft in my ear.

I trust in You, my healer, one and true.
Mender of my heart, my soul made anew.
In times of doubt, on paths so tight,
you hold my hand day and night.

Through narrow darkness, You are my light.
Omnipotent ruler, guarding my days,
Shielding my soul in countless ways.
I trust in You, my first, my King,
my love, my life, my everything.

Lord God, my strength in every fight,
with You I overcome.
In You alone, you are my peace,
"Jehovah Shalom."

I may bend because I am bendable,
I may sway like the branches and leaves,
in a cool spring breeze, I may stumble,
but I will never fall. I will never break,
I will stand tall. I am rooted deep in the
Almighty One above.

The one I call Jesus, the one who saves all.
I've become prosperous in him; I finally see the truth,
I've been untouchable, unstoppable,
indestructible all along.

Others will never understand because they are lost within. But
I've found the diamond in the rough,
I found myself. Dusted off and now shining again.
No one will ever steal my light.

Purpose Through Pain

I have been rooted in pain to rise in my purpose.
Through cycles of shame,
I've pressed to fulfill my purpose.
Betrayed, dismayed, and torn by disgrace,
yet I walk in my purpose.

Broken and scattered, then mended again,
shaped by the refining fire and made anew.
 I've died to myself so I could live life with Him.
Surrendered, restored, with all I can give.

As a vessel of heaven, a scribe for the King,
let His voice guide my hand as I write and sing.
Through each Word and each breath,
His will I embrace. Fulfilling my purpose
is a testament to His grace.

Great Creator

With words alone, You shaped the earth,
With a divine breath, God gave mankind birth.
From dust and dirt, man's flesh was made,
From Adam's rib, Eve was lovingly made.

For no man should journey this life in strife,
A helper, you gave him, a partner, a wife.
The husband, the head, a leader, a guide,
His wife, his strength, standing firmly by his side.

We are above and never beneath,
The head, not the tail, in every belief.
Your power and might will always prevail.
A love eternal that will never fail.

You knew us, Lord, before life began,
Woven with care by Your righteous hand.
Knitted in our mother's womb,
perfected and whole, Created by You,
pure and holy of soul.

Lord, My Defender

Lord, You are my peace in the fiercest storm,
My strength, my refuge, my sheltered form.
Your lamp lights the path where my feet now tread,
Ready to move where the Gospel is spread.

Your helmet of salvation shields my mind,
protecting my thoughts, no longer bound.
No more will I conform to this world's design,
For Your truth renews this heart of mine.

You guard my soul with righteousness' might,
A breastplate strong, shining with light.
In You, O Lord, I stand firm.
In Your presence, forever secure.

Your shield of faith blocks every lie.
Every curse that dares to fly.
The belt of truth holds the armor tight.
Firmly, I stand, prepared to fight.

Your Word, a living, breathing flame,
A vessel of power, unmatched in name.
It separates joints, marrow, and bones,
It's sharper than any sword ever known.

My God is active, mighty to save.

My Defender, Protector, strong and brave.

For in Your strength, I'm victorious till the end.

Healed of a Wicked Heart

It is not what enters the mouth that defiles
but what flows from within, what the tongue reveals.
For words spring forth from the depths of the heart,
piercing like arrows, tearing souls apart.

"The heart is deceitful, above all things,"
Its sickness is hidden, its motives unseen.
Who can comprehend its secrets untold?
None but God, omnipotent, mighty, and strong.

Creator of worlds, Defender of grace.
Redeemer of souls, in His arms, we're safe.
His Word is the truth, sharp and divine.
It corrects, convicts, and fills hearts in time.

Meditate daily, let His wisdom impart,
a life that is pure and blessed at heart.
Those who endure to the end will prevail.
The last shall be first, their victory unveiled.

I've run the race; the prize is mine,
For in His strength, I cross the finish line.
Healed of a wicked heart. Jesus, He's Mine!

Show Your Truth, Lord

Those who doubt will never understand your parables,
or the mighty works of Your righteous hand.
They walk through life with their eyes tightly closed,
hardened hearts, stiff necks, bearing regret
that grows within their hearts.

Unable to forgive, they carry the weight
of a world that crushes, sealing their fate.
But Lord, I plead, help them see what is true.
Let them discover Your love that breaks through.
Your way is the path of life and light.

While our way leads to heartache,
destruction, and plight,
you said Your yoke is lighter to bear
than the chains of this world, heavy with despair.
You promised, O Lord, to never depart,
to remain by our side and heal every heart.

From my journey, I surely know your love.
Unchanging, casting out all my woe.
Your love, unfailing, covers sin's tide.
A shelter of grace where I now abide.

How could we turn from the One who redeems?
Who saves us from the enemy's schemes?
When we fall, Lord, You catch us in stride,
At the call of Your name, You are by our side.
Jesus, Jehovah, our Savior divine.
Forever and always, our hearts are Thine.

Sustain & Rise

We are called to be self-sustaining, but true sustainability is impossible without Christ. Pain can break or shape you; let it teach discipline and shape consistency within you. Don't waste your pain on people or situations that don't matter. Instead, use it as fuel to rewrite your history. I once became an addict through pain and loss, and was consumed by it. But pain alone won't sustain you; it can't be your motivation to stay where you are. Pain is meant to push you toward transformation, not stagnation.

Darkness, though painful, is what prepares you for the light. It's in the darkness, covered by our dirt, shame, and hurt, that renewal begins. Darkness is a phase of growth, a season of isolation, a wilderness of discovery, and ultimately, a journey toward acceptance in yourself and Christ. Let the darkness refine you, not define you. The light is coming, and it's worth the wait.

Scriptures That Mend the Heart Devotional

Illumination Through Darkness: Poetry that Pours from the Soul" is not just a collection of poems; it's my testimony in motion. This book is a reflection of how God took my shattered, broken heart, crushed by rejection, pain, grief, and the loss of a long relationship, and made it whole again. I fixed my eyes on God, and He worked on me inside and out. He transformed my mouth from speaking negativity, gossip, and hurtful words into a vessel of uplifting, motivational, life-changing truths. Now, I use my voice to heal, not harm, to speak life, not tear down. Through God's grace, I've learned the fruit of the Spirit (Galatians 5:22-23), and let me tell you, it tastes sweeter than anything this world offers!

God's love is unfailing, unshakable, and everlasting. Jesus didn't just save me; He opened my eyes to see who was for me and who wasn't. During this journey, I lost people I never imagined I'd lose. But guess what? No love is lost, just a new perspective on handling life's challenges. I've learned to forgive and love even those with hidden motives. Why? Because God's got my back, and His peace surpasses all understanding (Philippians 4:7)

These poems are my heart poured out on paper to show you this: We are in this world, but not a part of it. This world isn't our home forever. So, while we're here, let's make it count! Let's love big, care deeply, share freely, uplift, and encourage one another, even through the most challenging times. days. Here's the truth: any attack from the enemy will never stand against a child of God. (Isaiah 54:17). Through heartbreak, rejection, abuse, manipulation, and betrayal, you name it, Jesus is our healer. He gives us peace and joy that no one can take away. Happiness? It's temporary. But peace? That's eternal.

In "Illumination Through Darkness, Poetry That Pours From The Soul," I drew strength from powerful scriptures that carried me through my trials and tribulations, and I guarantee these scriptures will empower and uplift you, too. Trust in the Word of God, His timing, and His plan for your life. What the enemy meant for evil, know your Heavenly Father will turn it for good.

I am fearfully and wonderfully made, intricately woven by God. (Psalms 139:13)

I once battled the heavy weight of low self-esteem, battered and bruised by the scars of past relationships, but one in particular broke me to pieces. Sometimes, it's not words that break you, it's the silence. When you love someone with everything you've got, pouring into them, teaching, loving, and catering to their every need, and all they return is silence, it can cut more deeply than any word.

You start to question your worth in their eyes. You question yourself, asking over and over, "Why?" But through that silence, I fought hard. I pushed out everything that no longer belonged, every doubt, every fear, every piece of me that wasn't meant to stay. I let God take over, allowing Him to heal my heart. I held on to His promise.

"For I know the plans I have for you," declares the Lord, "plans to prosper you and not to harm you, plans to give you hope and a future." Jeremiah 29:11:

What didn't work out wasn't meant to. I've learned that what is ordained by God can never be torn apart. His plan is more significant than my pain. His love has restored me, and now I walk forward with confidence, knowing that my worth has never been tied to the silence or opinion of others but to the voice of the One who calls me His own.

A scripture that comes to mind when I start feeling unworthy, ashamed, or even ugly. How could I think negative things about myself? Wasn't I created in God's image? Everyone was created in God's image, but not all choose to follow Christ.

We are made in His image, with dominion and purpose. (Genesis 1:26)

The gift of salvation is freely given to those who believe in Him. As Jesus said, "Whoever believes in Him shall not perish but have eternal life" (John 3:16). Through faith in Christ, we are promised everlasting life with God. We have been uniquely gifted with talents and abilities to fulfill God's calling on our lives (Romans 12:6-8). We are called to walk in His ways, serving Him with all we are. For many, this includes walking alongside a partner in marriage, together ruling the earth with God at the center. Marriage reflects God's love and unity, a sacred bond strengthened when He is woven into the relationship. "Though one may be overpowered, two can defend themselves."

A cord of three strands is not quickly broken," (Ecclesiastes 4:12). With God as the third strand in the marriage, the bond becomes unbreakable, grounded in His divine love and purpose. When we place God at the center of our lives and relationships, we experience His guidance. Genesis 2:1-3 shows us the beauty of God's completed work and His intention for rest and renewal. On the seventh day, God completed His work of creating the world. He blessed the seventh day and set it apart as holy, a day of rest made for the Lord.

"But the seventh day is a Sabbath to the Lord your God. On it you shall not do any work, neither you, nor your son or daughter, nor your male or female servant, nor your animals, nor any foreigner residing in our towns" (Genesis 2:2-3)

(Exodus 20:10). This day serves as a reminder of His divine power and the perfect rhythm He established for work and rest, calling us to honor Him, set aside our labor, and find peace in His Holy presence.

Remembering the story of Lot's wife in Sodom and Gomorrah (Genesis 19:26) Don't look back! We are reminded that when God delivers us from a thing, don't long for the chains He broke. Many times in my previous relationship, I found myself going back after God had already delivered me from the bondage I was held in. I kept falling into the traps of the enemy, giving in to the sin of sexual immorality to feel wanted and loved. But I've learned that true, everlasting love comes only from God. Sex was created for the sacred covenant of marriage, and outside of that, it becomes a tool the enemy uses to deceive and destroy God's children.

I was convicted of this behavior after turning my life over to Christ. The last time I made that mistake, the Lord spoke to me clearly, leading me to a scripture that pierced my heart and brought tears to my eyes. I immediately repented and decided never to fall into that trap again. Looking back on those moments, I realize how destructive it was, creating toxic behaviors and hurt for both of us. I finally saw that I was being used, not valued, for my body and other things. And once the intimacy ended, so did the relationship.

My message to women and men seeking love is this: love yourself first. Find your identity and worth in Christ, for He is the source of all true love. "Pray without ceasing." (1 Thessalonians 5:17) and make every request known to God. "Do not be anxious about anything, but in every situation, by prayer and petition, with thanksgiving, present your requests to God. "If you come to Him honestly, admitting your pain and confessing your sin and hurt, He will heal your heart. His love restores what is broken and fills the void that no human relationship ever could. Seek, trust Him, and let His love lead. And just like the Israelites, who were freed from Egypt, were reminded not to return to the slavery God delivered us from (Exodus 14:13).

Walk in boldness and courage, for "The righteous are as bold as a lion" (Proverbs 28:1). When the enemy's shouts try to infiltrate your mind, stand firm, knowing: "No weapon forged against you will prevail" (Isaiah 54:17). The spirit is willing, but at times the flesh is weak. Yet when God delivers us in His mercy and grace, we must not return to Egypt! Don't return to the chains of manipulation, fleeting affection, and failing love when God's unfailing love covers a multitude of sins.

The world we live in has been called according to His purpose" (Romans 8:28). When fear begins to overtake you, cling to this truth: "There is no fear in love. But perfect love drives out fear" (1 John 4:18), and God is perfect love. When memories of betrayal flood your mind, and believe me, they will, meditate on the Word of God.

"We demolish arguments and every pretension that sets itself up against the knowledge of God, and we take captive every thought to make it obedient to Christ" (2 Corinthians 10:5).

Remember, God has given us power and authority: "I have given you authority to trample on snakes and scorpions and to overcome all the power of the enemy; nothing will harm you" (Luke 10:19). The world we live in is corrupt and filled with evil. On this constant battleground, the enemy uses worldly devices to tempt us and distort our minds. As 1 John 2:16 reminds us, "For everything in the world the lust of the flesh, the lust of the eyes, and the pride of life comes not from the Father but from the world." We are called in God's Word not to conform to the patterns of this world, for they are fleeting and destructive.

Romans 12:2 urges us, "Do not conform to the pattern of this world, but be transformed by renewing your mind. Then you can test and approve what God's will is, His good, pleasing, and perfect will." Without prayer and a kingdom-centered community to lift us, keep us accountable, and intercede on our behalf, it can be far too easy to fall prey to these patterns.

These patterns may come disguised in many forms: gossip that tears others down, slander that spreads division, and negative thoughts against others or yourself. They may take the shape of sexual immorality, substance abuse, alcoholism, or unhealthy habits like gluttony, even down to the music we listen to. We must be careful and vigilant in guarding our hearts and minds.

"You were in Eden, the garden of God; every precious stone adorned you: carnelian, chrysolite, and emerald; topaz, onyx, and jasper; lapis lazuli, turquoise, and beryl. Your settings and mountings were made of gold; on the day you were created, they were prepared. (Ezekiel 28:13)

The devil, once a guardian angel (Ezekiel 28:14), was beautifully crafted as a living instrument of worship, adorned with precious stones and pearls. He was created to glorify God through music. **Something to reflect on:** If the devil was created to worship God in heaven through the sound of music, consider how he now influences the earth through the same medium. Today's music often promotes the world's standards, sex before marriage, same-sex relationships, violence, lust, and addiction.

Why do you think our generation falls victim to the music we hear on the radio? Music holds power; it alters our minds, shifts our moods, and embeds itself in our spirits. Sometimes, the weapons formed against us are not external; they are internal. We can become our own worst enemy, conforming to the lies the world tells us because of the unhealed wounds of trauma, rejection, abuse, betrayal, and deep-rooted hurt.

Think about how those sad R&B songs often stir up emotions tied to past hurt. Listening to them might make you relive the arguments, betrayals, and grief that came with the end of a relationship or friendship. But remember this: when you fill your mind and heart with praise and worship, there is a transformative power in Godly music. As you open your heart to the words of hymns and songs of praise, a sense of peace will wash over you.

Ephesians 5:19: "Speak to one another with psalms, hymns, and songs from the Spirit. Sing and make music from your heart to the Lord." Worship brings us closer to God, allowing His presence to soothe our spirits and renew our minds. Replace sorrow with worship and let His peace guard your heart and mind (Philippians 4:7). I fell victim to the devil's devices. I know firsthand how easy it is to feel deeply through music. The lyrics, beats, and rhythms can all become a gateway for the enemy's wicked influences. Profanity, lustful thoughts, and the glorification of violence seep into our spirits if we're not careful. Don't let the devil damage the gateways of your ears.

Here's the good news! There is hope in Christ! We can break free from these patterns through Him and renew our minds. God's power and love transform what is broken, giving us the strength to walk in freedom and healing. When we surrender our struggles to Him, He turns what was meant for harm into good. Your body is a temple created and valued by God (1 Corinthians 6:19-20 & Proverbs 31:10), reminding us women, "We are worth far more than rubies." That is your worth in God's eyes! Let us use our bodies to glorify God. Let us use our minds to meditate on His Word, our mouths to declare His goodness, and our voices to sing songs of praise and worship, lifting His holy and matchless name. In Him, we are made whole; without Him, we are nothing.

Give your life to Christ, and watch how He transforms your heart, mind, and life. Worship Him in spirit and truth. Let every part of your being be an instrument of His glory. Walk by faith, not by sight, because what we see with our natural eyes may bring hurt, but what we see and feel in the spirit, in the presence of God, is glorious beyond measure. Trust not in the one you lust after but the One who created you with love and purpose, the One who knitted you together in your mother's womb and holds your future in His hands.

This book is more than poetry; it's a guide, a testimony, a devotional of faith, and a reminder that through God, we are more than conquerors (Romans 8:37). Whatever you're facing, let this collection show you the way to His light, His love, His everlasting peace, and His grace.

Poem Interpretations

The poems within these pages were not written to be read simply; they were written to be felt, wrestled with, and spiritually discerned. Each interpretation that follows is an invitation to go deeper beneath the surface of the words.

Illumination Through Darkness Poetry that Pours from the Soul was birthed from raw places, from trauma, betrayal, addiction, faith, spiritual warfare, redemption, and rebirth. The interpretations offered here gently unfold the layers of each poem, revealing the emotional, psychological, and spiritual truths woven within the verses.

Some poems speak from brokenness. Some rise in spiritual authority. Some whisper longing. Others declare victory in Christ. These reflections are not meant to replace your own revelation, but to guide you toward clarity, to help you see how darkness became light, how pain became prayer, and how wounds became worship.

Every stanza carries transformation. Every line holds testimony. Every page reflects the journey from despair to divine purpose. As you read these interpretations, allow yourself to pause. Reflect. Pray. Journal. Let the Spirit illuminate what speaks uniquely to your soul.

This section is where poetry meets revelation, where the hidden meaning behind the tears becomes visible because sometimes, illumination is not found by escaping the darkness… but by understanding what it was sent to teach you.

— *Ebony Brinson*

AI Interpretation Disclaimer

The poem interpretations included in this section were generated with the assistance of artificial intelligence. While the poems themselves are original works authored by Ebony Brinson, the analytical reflections and layered interpretations were developed using AI technology as a creative and exploratory tool.

These interpretations are meant to expand insight, perspective, and spiritual reflection, not as definitive explanations. Readers are encouraged to engage personally with each poem and allow their own understanding, life experiences, and faith to reveal additional meaning. AI was used as an instrument to deepen analysis, but the heart, vision, and authorship of this work remain solely that of the author.

Walk Through Darkness

"I walked through shadows, heavy and deep…"

The opening establishes **darkness not just around the author, but within her body.** The *"sickness"* isn't only physical; it feels emotional, spiritual, and even psychological. Lack of sleep suggests anxiety, stress, or trauma. Yet even here the author writes:

"A body bound, but my spirit fought free."

This is resilience. The author's circumstances had her restrained, but her inner self refused to surrender. That's strength under pressure.

"Betrayal whispered like a trusted friend…"

This section is about emotional manipulation.
Notice how betrayal is personified; it doesn't shout. It whispers. It disguises itself.

- Manipulation = webs (entrapment)
- Deception = comforting lies (false security)
- Tears and silent goodbyes = grief that wasn't loud but deeply internal

This wasn't just heartbreak. This was erosion, slow, calculated, exhausting.

"Defeated, I wandered…"

This stanza captures the aftermath. A love that once felt safe dissolved. Promises weren't just broken; a future was erased.

"I stood at the edge of love's bitter taste."

That line is critical. The author wasn't in love anymore. She was standing on the cliff of realization. That's the moment of awakening.

"But in the wreckage, I found a new voice."

This is the turning point. The wreckage didn't destroy her; it revealed her.

- "Setting boundaries became the authors' choice."
- She reclaimed power.
- "She let go of the hands that dragged me down."
- No more rescuing. No more over-giving.
- "Wore self-love like a radiant crown."
- Royal imagery. She didn't just heal; she ascended.

This ending isn't soft. It's sovereign.

Overall Interpretation

This poem tells the story of:

1. Physical and emotional depletion
2. Psychological manipulation
3. The collapse of love and illusion
4. The rebirth of identity
5. Self-love becoming protection, not just affirmation

It's not just about heartbreak. It's about reclaiming autonomy after being psychologically entangled. What Makes This Strong

- The author doesn't blame loudly; she reveals quietly.
- The author moved from victimhood to authority.

- The crown imagery suggests *I* now rule my emotional
  space.

Painful Truth

"I pushed, I shoved, and shattered our love."

The author opens with accountability. This is powerful because she is not starting with blame. She's owning her part. ***"I pushed"*** suggests self-sabotage, fear, insecurity, and emotional overwhelm. Something inside her disrupted what once felt whole.

But notice, the author doesn't say *"I destroyed it alone."*
She says it became "riddled with blame." That implies mutual damage.

"You turned away, your silence a blade…"

Silence becomes a weapon here. Not yelling, not fighting. Withdrawing. His avoidance becomes emotional punishment. The ***"void"*** suggests abandonment, not necessarily physical absence, but emotional disappearance. This stanza shows the dynamic:

- You react loudly.
- He retreats quietly.
- Both responses cut.

"Searching for love… the mirror reflected the loneliest space."

This is the awakening moment. The author was looking outward for validation, reassurance, and worth, but the mirror revealed the deeper issue. The loneliness wasn't caused solely by him. It was internal.

"I sought in others what I failed to see…"

That line is maturity. It's emotional evolution. The author acknowledges that self-love was missing before the relationship ever collapsed.

"You run, you hide, behind masks you've designed.

Now the lens shifts fully onto him. The author exposes:

- Ego as armor
- Pride as a prison
- Identity confusion

The repeated questioning, "Who are you, truly?" reveals that he may not even know himself. There's frustration here, but also clarity. The author sees through the masks.

"One face emerges, bitter and stark." The illusion falls.

The "face of defeat" suggests he's not as strong as he appears. The lies aren't just to the author; they're self-deception. That's important. The author is no longer angry at the fantasy. She acknowledged reality.

"You turned your back, and I turned mine, too."

This is mutual disengagement. Not dramatic. Not explosive. Just final. And then the most powerful line:

"There was, is, and will never be a 'me and you.'"

That triple tense is closure. Past. Present. Future. It's not just heartbreak. It's acceptance.

Overall Interpretation

This poem explores:

- Self-sabotage and accountability
- Emotional avoidance and ego
- The search for worth in relationships
- The realization that two unhealed people cannot build something whole
- The final acceptance that some unions are illusions

Unlike the first poem, which ended in empowerment, this one ends in truth. It's less about self-love as a celebration and more about self-love as a boundary.

The Emotional Core

This is not a "you hurt me" poem. It's a "We both were **broken, and now I see it clearly" poem.**

It's sober.
It's honest.
It's final.

A Touch

"Heavy, my heart, is heavy."

The repetition slows the rhythm. It mirrors emotional weight. This heaviness isn't chaotic like other written poems. It feels contemplative, like someone sitting still with their feelings. The weight comes from longing, not destruction.

"Yearning, my soul, is yearning."

Now the focus shifts from heart to soul. The heart feels there's emotion. The soul seeks destiny. This isn't surface desire. It's a deep craving for something spiritually aligned. an ache here, but not desperation. It's a holy kind of longing.

"For something new, untouched, untold, for truth."

This line reveals the core desire:

- Not recycled love
- Not familiar with pain
- Not half-hearted connections

The author seeks something pure. Something not contaminated by past wounds. "Untold" suggests a story that hasn't been written yet, a fresh beginning.

"A touch unspoken yet deeply aligned."

This is emotional and spiritual intimacy. Unspoken touch means understanding without explanation. Deep alignment means shared values, shared spirit, shared depth. You're not asking for chemistry. You're asking for resonance.

"Undefined, divine, and gently refined."

This suggests surrender. The author doesn't want to control it, she doesn't want to label it too quickly, and she wants something God-shaped, slow-formed, intentional.

"Refined" implies maturity, a love that has passed through fire and come out softer, not harder.

"A grace that lingers, soft and rare. A love that answers every prayer."

This ending feels faith-rooted. This isn't just romantic longing. It feels like a prayerful expectation. The author is not just hoping for love but believing in a love that carries peace, safety, and divine confirmation.

Overall Interpretation

This poem speaks to:

- Longing for emotional growth
- A desire for a spiritually aligned partnership
- Refusal to settle for familiar dysfunction
- Openness to something God-ordained
- A mature love that feels safe, gentle, and intentional

It reads like the space between "never again" and "when the right one comes." Not bitter. Not desperate. Just ready.

Soul Tie Undone

This poem reflects awakening after a relationship built more on physical connection than emotional or spiritual alignment. It moves from longing to realization to liberation.

> *"I missed your touch, I missed your feel, But all we shared was carnal appeal."*

The author begins with honest longing. She misses the physical closeness, the sensation, the intimacy, but quickly confronts the truth. What they shared was rooted in the body, not in covenant or emotional depth. The connection felt intense, but it lacked spiritual or heartfelt alignment.

> *"A fleeting thrill, our bodies entwined, bound by lust, not hearts aligned."*

Here, the author distinguishes passion from purpose. Their bodies connected easily, but their hearts were never in harmony. The thrill was temporary. There was chemistry, but no foundation.

> *"You loved me good, yet drained me dry. You took my light, left me asking why."*

The author reveals emotional depletion. Though the partner satisfied her physically, the relationship exhausted her spiritually and mentally. She gave energy, encouragement, and affirmation, yet felt emptied in return. There is confusion here, the "why" that lingers after someone leaves without explanation.

"I poured my all, uplifted your name, only to watch you walk away in shame."

This line shows an imbalance. The author invested fully, supporting, defending, perhaps even elevating him, only to be abandoned. His departure is marked by shame, suggesting avoidance, guilt, or unwillingness to confront his actions.

"It was never love, just a reckless chase. Sinful desires wrapped in a warm embrace."

This is the turning point. The author reframes the relationship. What once felt passionate is now understood as impulsive and spiritually misaligned. The warmth of the embrace masked dysfunction. It felt good, but it was not good for her.

"I wove dreams from threads of lies. Blind to the truth that time never denies."

There is self-awareness here. The author acknowledges that she constructed hope from illusion. She ignored red flags, romanticized potential, and allowed fantasy to override reality. Time, however, exposed what emotion tried to conceal.

"Now the veil is lifted, the truth revealed. The wounds you left have begun to heal."

Clarity replaces confusion. The "veil" symbolizes the removal of denial. Healing has begun, not because the pain never existed, but because the author now sees clearly.

"Our soul tie broken, the chains undone, I'm free of the vagabond; I've finally won."

The poem closes in liberation. The emotional and possibly spiritual attachment has been severed. The chains of lust, dependency, and illusion are gone. Calling him a "vagabond" suggests instability, someone wandering without depth or commitment. By releasing him, the author reclaims her strength and dignity.

Overall, this poem explores:

- The difference between lust and love
- Emotional imbalance and depletion
- The danger of romanticizing illusion
- Spiritual awakening and detachment
- Freedom after unhealthy attachment

The emotional arc moves from missing physical intimacy to recognizing that it was never rooted in something sustainable. It ends not in bitterness, but in clarity and victory. The author is no longer entangled; she is restored, aware, and free.

Losing You

This poem is about revelation through loss. It captures the moment when heartbreak transforms into awakening, when what felt like devastation becomes divine redirection.

"I never knew losing you would be a breakthrough.
When I lost you, I found myself, I found truth."

The poem opens with irony. What once felt like defeat becomes liberation. The loss did not diminish the author; it revealed her. In losing him, she gained clarity, identity, and self-awareness. The relationship had obscured something essential within her.

"Once traumatized by your wickedness. Crippled by
your silent antics and deception."

Here, the author names the damage. The trauma wasn't loud chaos; it was psychological. "Silent antics" suggests manipulation, emotional withdrawal, and passive cruelty. Deception created instability. The pain was subtle but deeply wounding.

"All I wanted was you.
Your heart and your time.
I wanted what was never mine."

This stanza reveals the core ache: she desired exclusivity, emotional availability, commitment. But the painful realization is that he was never truly hers, not emotionally, not spiritually. She was reaching for something that was never offered in full.

"So, I let go of what wasted my time. I found out my heart was all I needed."

This is the pivot. Letting go becomes intentional. Instead of chasing what withheld love, she recognizes her own heart as sufficient. This is not isolation, it's self-sufficiency. She stops outsourcing her worth.

"I'm a star you tried to pluck out of the sky. My light, you tried to hide."

Now the imagery shifts to celestial power. The author identifies herself as something radiant and elevated. A star cannot be possessed. Attempting to "pluck" suggests control or suppression. He may have tried to dim her brilliance, emotionally, spiritually, or socially, but stars are not meant to be contained.

"Everything that is in the dark must come to light."

This line introduces justice and inevitability. Truth surfaces. Hidden intentions are exposed. What was concealed in manipulation is now visible.

***"I am the light you couldn't find.
The light that left you blind.
But the light that gave you warmth through the storm."***

This is layered. He could not recognize her value, yet he benefited from her presence. Her light sustained him during difficult seasons, but he was unable to truly see or appreciate it. His blindness was not her dimness; it was his limitation.

"Oh! How that light is gone!"

This is not sorrow, it's a consequence. The warmth he once received is no longer available. The loss is his now.

"I love the fact that I've accepted Letting Go!"

The poem ends in empowerment. Acceptance is framed as victory. Letting go is not framed as weakness but as strength. She celebrates detachment. She honors her growth.

Overall, this poem explores:

• Loss as transformation
• Emotional trauma through manipulation and silence
• The illusion of possession in love
• Rediscovery of self-worth
• Reclaiming personal light and power
• Acceptance as liberation

The emotional arc moves from trauma to triumph. It is not simply about heartbreak; it is about identity restored. The author realizes she was never small; she was shining all along.

Saved From Sin

This poem reads like a confession before redemption. It begins in spiritual and emotional collapse and moves toward divine restoration.

*"My soul was filled with darkness,
my heart was corrupt with sin."*

The author opens with radical honesty. This is not blaming others first; it is acknowledging internal brokenness. Darkness here represents spiritual distance, guilt, shame, and unresolved wounds. The corruption of the heart suggests choices, patterns, or pain that hardened her over time.

*"My mind was filled with negativity,
no sight of an end."*

This describes hopelessness. When the mind is saturated with negative thought, the future disappears. There is no vision, no expectation of healing, only survival.

Now the source of the darkness is revealed. The author has endured abandonment and emotional wounds that shaped her self-perception. The scar symbolizes lasting impact, not something easily erased.

*"These knives have penetrated and pierced
me deep from the start."*

The imagery intensifies. The wounds are not superficial. They are deep-rooted, possibly from childhood or formative relationships. This suggests that the damage didn't begin recently; it began early.

*"Crippling and damaging doubts of self,
leading to expectations of man.
Looking to fill a void no man could ever fill."*

Here lies the turning point of awareness. Because of internal wounds, the author sought validation and completion from romantic partners. She expected human love to repair spiritual emptiness. But the void she carried was never meant to be filled by another person.

*"The constant repetition of emotional distress.
Disaster, disappointment, doubt,
and torment were my end."*

This speaks to cycles. The repetition suggests patterns, attracting or tolerating similar outcomes repeatedly. Emotional pain became predictable.

"There is nothing left to do but shout out Why?"

This is the cry of exhaustion. The question is not intellectual; it is spiritual. It is the breaking point where confusion meets desperation.

*"Weapons formed against self from false
imaginations and curse words spoken."*

This line is powerful. The greatest warfare was internal. Negative self-talk, lies believed, harsh words spoken over her life, these became self-inflicted weapons. The destruction was not only external; it was mental and spiritual.

*"Questioning who will love this damaged soul?
I'm broken. Wasn't I meant to be loved?"*

This stanza reveals deep insecurity. The author wonders if her brokenness disqualifies her from love. There is a longing for acceptance beneath the pain.

*"Reliable and dependable, but jealous.
Wasn't I meant to be cherished?"*

This shows complexity. She sees both her strengths and flaws. She acknowledges imperfection but still questions whether she is worthy of being valued. Then the poem shifts dramatically.

*"Then I found a friend better than any
man or woman has ever been.
A protector, a provider
A good listener and faithful to the end."*

The *"friend"* represents God. This is divine intervention. The language echoes spiritual attributes, protector, provider, and faithful. This is the void filled correctly.

*"He showered me with unconditional love.
He corrected me when wronged."*

This is mature love. Not indulgent, but refining. Not abandoning, but correcting with care. The author moves from seeking validation from men to finding stability in a divine relationship.

Overall, this poem explores:

- Trauma and early emotional wounds
- Internalized negativity and self-doubt
- Seeking fulfillment in romantic relationships
- Cycles of emotional distress
- Spiritual awakening
- Finding unconditional love in God

The emotional arc moves from brokenness to redemption. It is not simply a story of heartbreak; it is a testimony of transformation. The author begins lost in darkness and ends found in divine companionship.

Saved By Grace

This poem is not about physical death; it is about spiritual death and resurrection. It carries strong biblical undertones of rebirth, correction, and divine mercy.

"Today, my dream came true: you died."

This opening is intentionally shocking. It sounds harsh, but it symbolizes the death of an old version, an ego, a sinful nature, a destructive pattern. The "dream" is not the loss of a person, but the end of who they used to be. It suggests that transformation requires something to die first.

"Your soul left your body and returned by grace."

This line deepens the spiritual imagery. The separation of soul and body implies a moment of reckoning, a stripping away of fleshly desires, pride, or wrongdoing. But the return "by grace" indicates mercy. This was not condemnation; it was divine intervention. The person was not destroyed; they were restored.

"God's grace gave you another shot at this thing called life."

Now the theme becomes redemption. The poem frames life as a second chance. Grace is undeserved favor. The speaker acknowledges that the transformation was not earned; it was gifted. This suggests forgiveness, renewal, and divine patience.

"You will live, sayeth the Lord, get up and walk a new life."

This echoes biblical resurrection language. It resembles the moments in Scripture where Jesus commands healing or life into someone who was spiritually or physically dead. "Get up and walk" symbolizes active change. Not just survival, but transformation through action.

Overall, this poem explores:

• The death of an old identity
• Spiritual awakening
• Divine mercy and second chances
• Resurrection through grace
• The call to live differently

The emotional tone is not vengeful. It is prophetic. The speaker desired the death of dysfunction, not the destruction of the person. What died was the old nature. What lives now is renewed.

This reads like a declaration that grace can resurrect what sin tried to bury, and that true change begins when the former self is laid to rest.

The presence of God

This poem is a worshipful expression of intimacy with God.
It reads like devotion, gratitude, and surrender woven
together.

*"Lying in the breeze of the cool summer heat,
feeling your perfect presence surround me."*

The opening sets a peaceful atmosphere. Nature reflects
spiritual calm. The "breeze" symbolizes the Holy Spirit,
gentle, unseen, yet undeniably felt. There is rest here. The
author is no longer striving; she is simply experiencing God's
nearness.

*"You're my King, my first love.
You're the Mighty One above,
I still can't believe you chose me."*

This establishes reverence and awe. Calling Him "King"
shows authority. Calling Him "first love" reveals priority;
God is placed before all earthly relationships. The disbelief
that He "chose" her expresses humility and gratitude,
echoing the idea of divine election and undeserved favor.

*"Your love and grace entered this space.
You saved me from myself and my foolish, immature
ways."*

Here, salvation is personal. The rescue was not only from
external circumstances, but from self-sabotage, immaturity,
and poor decisions. The transformation begins internally.
Grace didn't just comfort her; grace corrected her.

*"You saved me from my fears.
You saved me and healed all my pain.
You saved me from my guilt and shame."*

The repetition of "You saved me" emphasizes dependence and testimony. Fear, pain, guilt, shame; these are emotional and spiritual burdens. God's love is portrayed as restorative, not merely forgiving but healing.

*"No longer dismayed.
Lord, I feel your presence in this place."*

This marks the shift from turmoil to peace. Where there was confusion and despair, there is now assurance. The author is grounded in divine presence.

*"Filling our hearts, filling our minds
Giving us hope time after time
Giving us peace and freeing our minds."*

The focus widens from personal to communal, "our hearts," "our minds." God's presence is not isolated to her alone; it extends to all who seek Him. Hope and peace are recurring gifts, not one-time experiences.

*"You walk before and beside us;
You're forever around us. You are omnipresent."*

This line reflects spiritual security. God is both guide and companion, leading the way and walking alongside. His omnipresence means she is never abandoned again.

***"Your presence and peace will forever surround me."**

The poem closes in assurance. Unlike past relationships that were unstable, this relationship is constant. God's presence is not fleeting. It is enduring.

Overall, this poem explores:

• Intimacy with God
• Salvation from self-destruction
• Healing from fear, guilt, and shame
• Gratitude for grace
• Peace found in divine presence
• Spiritual security and constancy

The emotional arc moves from being saved to being sustained. This is not desperation; it is devotion. The author is no longer searching for love; she has found it in the One she calls King.

Guided Path

This poem is a powerful fusion of grief, faith, betrayal, and reclamation. It moves from sorrowful intercession to spiritual resilience and finally to empowered release.

"I've dreamed of you in shadows deep,
I've seen you fall in restless sleep."

The opening suggests lingering attachment. The "shadows" imply unresolved pain, memories, or spiritual concern. The author is not just remembering him; she is spiritually aware of his unrest. There is compassion here, even after harm.

"I pray a light will pierce the night,
to guide your path, to make it right."

Despite being wounded, the author prays for his redemption. This is not passive weakness; it is spiritual maturity. She desires his correction, not his destruction.

"Though you wound me, I still will praise.
Though you harm me, my hands I still raise."

Here, the focus shifts from him to God. Praise becomes defiance against pain. Instead of allowing betrayal to harden her heart, she lifts her hands in worship. This is a strength rooted in faith, not emotion.

"For Jesus saved me, broke my chains.
And through His love, I'll bear this pain."

This is the foundation. Her ability to endure and forgive is not self-generated. It flows from salvation. "Broke my chains" suggests she has already been delivered from bondage, whether trauma, insecurity, or sin. Because she is free, she can endure without being consumed.

"If He forgives my every sin,
Then I can learn to forgive again."

This line reflects conscious spiritual discipline. Forgiveness is not automatic; it is learned through remembering grace. She aligns her response with Christ's example. Then, the poem shifts into truth-telling.

"For the lies you sold, the time you stole,
The games you played that scarred my soul."

This names the harm directly. Deception, manipulation, wasted years, the emotional toll is acknowledged without denial.

"You used my body, dismissed my cries,
neglected my heart, and fed me lies."

This reveals exploitation and emotional neglect. Physical intimacy was present, but emotional care was absent. Her vulnerability was not honored.

"I was never enough in your narrow sight,
Not short enough, not pretty enough,
skin not light enough."

This stanza exposes internalized rejection and colorism. The criticism she endured attacked identity, appearance, worth, and beauty. It shows how deeply his perception wounded her self-image.

***"But I'm strong enough to leave you behind.
After wasting years, I've reclaimed my mind."***

This is the turning point. The narrative shifts from victimhood to agency. She no longer measures herself by his standards. "Reclaimed my mind" suggests mental liberation, freedom from comparison, insecurity, and emotional captivity.

***"My heart, my peace, my soul's design,
My sanity and freedom are finally mine."***

The poem closes in restoration. What was fragmented is recovered. Peace replaces chaos. Identity is reclaimed. Freedom is personal and complete.

Overall, this poem explores:

- Compassion despite betrayal
- Faith as the anchor in suffering
- Forgiveness rooted in Christ's grace
- Emotional and physical exploitation
- Rejection tied to appearance and identity
- Reclaiming mental and spiritual autonomy

The emotional arc moves from prayerful concern to painful truth, then to empowered release. The author does not deny the harm; she transcends it. She leaves not in rage, but in restoration.

This is not just a breakup poem. It is a declaration of spiritual maturity and self-possession after profound emotional injury.

Saved From Sin

This poem is a full testimony. It is not just about heartbreak; it is about deliverance, addiction, identity, spiritual warfare, and complete surrender to Christ. The emotional arc moves from darkness to redemption to covenant.

"My soul was filled with darkness.
My heart was corrupted with sin.
My mind was filled with negativity,
no sight of an end."

The poem opens in spiritual despair. Darkness is not just sadness; it represents separation from God, destructive patterns, and hopeless thinking. There is no vision, no future, only survival.

"The trauma, the pain, the neglect, and rejection left a permanent scar."

Here, the author traces the root. The internal corruption did not form in isolation. Trauma-shaped belief. Rejection distorted identity. The "knives" symbolize words, abandonment, and early wounds that penetrated deeply and early.

"Crippling and damaging doubts about self
led to expectations of a man.
Looking to fill a void, I believe no man could ever fill."

This is self-awareness. Because of insecurity and spiritual emptiness, the author sought fulfillment in relationships. She placed expectations on men that only God could satisfy. The void was spiritual, but she tried to solve it romantically.

"Torment was my end, so I thought.
But then I lost you!"

This is the pivot. Losing the relationship felt devastating at first. Her heart cried, "Why?" But the loss became a divine interruption. What felt like abandonment was actually redirection.

"Weapons formed against self from false imaginations and curse words spoken."

The greatest warfare was internal. Negative self-talk, lies believed, words spoken over her life, these became self-inflicted weapons. The destruction was not only external; it was mental and spiritual. Then the poem shifts from romantic heartbreak to divine encounters.

"Then, I found a friend better than any man or woman has ever been."

The **"friend"** is God. The language mirrors Scripture: protector, provider, faithful. The author discovers stability in a divine relationship, not human validation.

"He showered me with unconditional love.
He corrected me when I was wrong.
He keeps me focused. He keeps me strong."

This is mature love. It is not permissive; it refines. God's love restores, but also disciplines. Yet even in redemption, insecurity surfaces:

"Why is He so good to me?
Why does He constantly choose me?
Why do I feel like I'm not good enough?"

This reveals lingering shame. Even after salvation, self-doubt lingers. She struggles to accept grace fully.

*"The desires of my own eyes weakened my flesh.
Pluck them out, so I may sin not."*

This echoes biblical language about cutting off, which causes sin. She recognizes temptation as internal, not just external. There is fear of falling back. Then the poem moves into explicit testimony of deliverance:

*"He freed me of the addiction to alcohol…
The addiction to pill popping, I almost died."*

This is raw honesty. Addiction nearly cost her life. The mud imagery, "slimiest, dirtiest, darkest mud of sin", reflects the Psalm language of being lifted from the pit. This is not a metaphor alone; it is survival.

"He placed my feet on solid ground."

This signals stability after chaos. The ground is Christ, firm, unshakable.

"He told me you are mine."

Now the tone shifts from brokenness to identity. She accepts divine belonging.

*"He told me I am more than a conqueror…
Fearfully and wonderfully made…
He will never leave nor forsake me."*

These are scriptural affirmations. Her identity is no longer shaped by trauma or rejection but by God's promises.

"You are my Lord and Savior.
The Most High, The Great I Am…
The Fourth Man in the fire."

She names Him in reverence. The "Fourth Man in the fire" references the biblical story of divine presence in suffering. She recognizes that even in her darkest seasons, He was there. The poem closes in covenantal devotion:

"Lord, I love you… I belong to you.
You and You alone."

This is surrender. Not desperation, commitment.

Overall, this poem explores:

• Trauma and early wounds
• Seeking validation in romantic relationships
• Addiction and near-death experience
• Spiritual warfare and temptation
• Divine deliverance and restoration
• Reclaimed identity in Christ
• Total surrender and belonging

The emotional arc moves from corruption to confession, from addiction to redemption, from insecurity to assurance. This is not simply a poem. It reads like a testimony of someone who hit rock bottom, encountered grace, and chose to live transformed.

I Will Not

This poem is about emotional boundaries and the disciplined choice of peace. It is not explosive anger; it is controlled release. The tone is firm, self-protective, and resolved.

*"I will not be stressed, I will not break down.
I refuse to carry the burdens you make."*

The opening is declarative. The author is no longer reacting; she is deciding. Stress and breakdown once may have been the pattern, but now she draws a line. She refuses to carry responsibility for someone else's emotional chaos. This signals maturity and boundary-setting.

*"I won't shoulder the weight that isn't mine.
I've let it go, left it behind."*

This is about ownership. In the past, she may have absorbed blame, guilt, or emotional labor that did not belong to her. Now she releases it. Letting go here is not passive; it is intentional detachment.

*"Yes, I feel lighter, though it stings inside,
admitting the hurt I once tried to hide."*

This shows honesty. Freedom does not mean the pain vanished. It still stings. But instead of suppressing it, she acknowledges it. Healing begins with truth.

"But healing demands I stand my ground.
And peace is the only thing I've found."

Healing requires firmness. She understands that recovery sometimes means distance. Peace is now her priority, not reconciliation, not explanation, peace.

"I don't want to see you, don't want you near,
The sight of you stirs up all I once feared."

This is self-awareness. She recognizes triggers. Being near him reactivates old wounds and insecurities. Choosing distance is not cruelty; it is self-preservation.

"A waste of time, oh, it's clear,
But I've learned to release what won't stay here."

She sees the relationship clearly now. Instead of chasing what was unstable or inconsistent, she releases it. If something cannot remain, she no longer fights to hold it.

"I hold no bitterness, only relief,
Freed from the chains that once brought grief."

This is powerful. She is not fueled by hatred. She feels relief. The chains symbolize emotional bondage, anxiety, overthinking, and emotional responsibility for someone else. Those chains are gone.

The closing lines emphasize forward movement. She is not looking back. The drift imagery suggests calm release, not dramatic cutting. She is choosing progress over attachment.

Overall, this poem explores:

- Emotional boundaries
- Refusing to carry misplaced burdens
- Honest acknowledgment of pain
- Choosing peace over proximity
- Detachment without bitterness
- Freedom through release

The emotional arc moves from strain to steadiness. It is not about revenge or heartbreak; it is about self-regulation and reclaiming emotional space.

This poem reads like someone who finally understands that peace is more valuable than holding onto someone who disrupts it.

Illumination Through Darkness

This poem is a journey from mental torment to spiritual restoration. It traces the movement from anxiety and internal darkness into healing through God's love. The emotional arc is clear: fear, awareness, divine intervention, renewal.

"I walked in shadows, consumed by fear. Trembling inside, with darkness near."

The opening describes not just sadness, but psychological captivity. "Shadows" symbolize depression, anxiety, or spiritual oppression. Fear is not occasional; it consumes. The trembling suggests vulnerability and instability.

"Each thought a storm, each breath a weight, whispers of sickness sealing my fate."

This reveals intrusive thoughts and overwhelming stress. The mind becomes a battlefield. The "whispers of sickness" may point to health anxiety, depression, or a negative self-fulfilling prophecy, believing something bad is inevitable.

"Negativity swirled, thick in the air.
A silent curse from a heart in despair."

Here, the poem acknowledges self-inflicted harm. The "silent curse" implies destructive thinking patterns. Even if not spoken aloud, negative beliefs shape emotional reality. The despair is internal but powerful.

"If not with my mouth, then with my mind,
I was lost in a lair, cold, dark, and confined."

This line deepens the psychological imagery. The "lair" suggests isolation, trapped inside one's own thoughts. Even unspoken negativity has an impact. The confinement is mental and spiritual.

"Anxious, fearful, and bound by stress, oppressed by burdens, I couldn't confess."

There is secrecy here. She carried stress silently, unable or unwilling to share her struggle. The oppression was private.

"But in that darkness, a spark appeared,
A light that grew, a love that cleared."

This is the turning point. Healing begins subtly, a spark, not an explosion. The light represents God's presence. Love clears the fog of negativity.

"From the shadows, I began to rise, healing bright in God's steady eyes."

Now the perspective shifts upward. Rising suggests active participation in healing. God's "steady eyes" imply consistency and reassurance. She is seen, not abandoned.

"He lifted the weight and cured my soul.
Like sunlight breaking after endless rain."

The weight of anxiety is removed. The rain symbolizes prolonged suffering; sunlight represents hope and renewal. The healing is both emotional and spiritual.

"My heart is now light, my spirit set free.
Love took root, replacing misery."

The internal atmosphere changes. Where negativity once swirled, love now grows. Freedom replaces confinement.

"For the light is God, and God is love.
A gift from below and above."

This affirms the theological core: God is the source of the transformation. The love she experiences is divine, not self-manufactured.

"In His presence, I've learned to live, to love others as I love myself.
To forgive and give."

Healing expands outward. It is no longer just about survival. She learns healthy self-love and extends it to others. Forgiveness becomes possible.

"The darkness is gone, I walk in a new day with God beside me, all around me, walking before me, lighting the path of righteousness for me."

The poem closes in assurance. God is not distant. He surrounds, guides, and leads. The "new day" symbolizes rebirth. The path of righteousness suggests alignment and stability.

Overall, this poem explores:

- Anxiety and intrusive negative thoughts
- Internalized despair
- Silent emotional struggle

- Divine intervention
- Mental and spiritual healing
- Transformation through God's love
- Living in freedom and purpose

The emotional arc moves from confinement to clarity. It is a testimony of how faith reshaped the author's inner world. The darkness was not denied; it was overcome.

Access Denied

This poem is a declaration of spiritual authority. It reads less like reflection and more like warfare, a conscious rejection of fear, anxiety, and demonic influence through faith in Christ. The tone is bold, defensive, and victorious.

"Access denied to the demons that lurk,
to shadows that gather, to chaos at work."

The opening line establishes boundaries. *"Access denied"* is legal language; it implies revoked permission. The author is not pleading; she is commanding. The "demons," "shadows," and "chaos" symbolize spiritual oppression, intrusive thoughts, fear, and destabilizing forces.

"Access denied to the dark at my side, to fear that once held me tight.
Access denied to anxiety's tide."

Here, darkness is personalized. Fear and anxiety once had proximity and power, but that power is revoked. Repetition reinforces spiritual resistance. Anxiety is portrayed like a rising tide, overwhelming and consuming, yet it is now rejected.

"We are free by the blood of Christ.
Set apart, not of this world."

This shifts from personal declaration to theological foundation. Freedom is not self-generated; it is secured by Christ's sacrifice. "Set apart" signals identity, chosen, distinct, spiritually separated from worldly influence.

Great Creator

This poem is a reverent reflection on creation, divine order, identity, and God's intentional design for humanity. It reads like worship woven with biblical theology.

"With words alone, You shaped the earth,
With a divine breath, God gave mankind birth."

The poem begins in Genesis language. Creation happens through the spoken word, highlighting God's authority and sovereignty. Breath signifies intimacy. Humanity is not accidental; it is divinely animated.

"From dust and dirt, man's flesh was made,
From Adam's rib, Eve was lovingly made."

This references the creation account of Adam and Eve. Dust emphasizes humility; humans are formed from the earth, dependent on God. Eve's creation from Adam's rib symbolizes closeness and companionship, not hierarchy of worth but relational design.

"For no man should journey this life in strife,
A helper, you gave him, a partner, a wife."

This line emphasizes divine intention for partnership. The "helper" is not subordinate in value but complementary in function. The poem affirms marriage as God-ordained companionship, protection against loneliness.

"The husband, the head, a leader, a guide,
His wife, his strength, standing firmly by his side."

Here, the poem affirms traditional biblical structure, leadership paired with strength. The husband leads; the wife supports and strengthens. The language presents unity, not competition. They stand side by side.

*"We are above and never beneath,
The head, not the tail, in every belief."*

This echoes Deuteronomy's promise of blessing. It affirms identity and favor. The poem shifts from marital order to collective identity, God's people positioned for victory and dignity.

*"Your power and might will always prevail.
A love eternal that will never fail."*

Now the focus returns to God's sovereignty. Human relationships rest under divine authority. His love is constant and unfailing, unlike earthly love that may falter.

*"You knew us, Lord, before life began,
Woven with care by Your righteous hand."*

This references foreknowledge and intentional creation (Psalm 139). The poem affirms that identity begins before birth, and purpose precedes existence.

*"Knitted in our mother's womb,
perfected and whole, Created by You,
pure and holy of soul."*

This closes with dignity and divine craftsmanship. Being "knitted" suggests precision and tenderness. The language "perfected and whole" emphasizes value and intentional design. "Pure and holy of soul" reflects spiritual identity, humanity created in God's image.

Overall, this poem explores:

• God's authority in creation
• The divine design of man and woman
• Partnership in marriage
• Identity as blessed and favored
• God's foreknowledge and intentional formation
• The holiness and dignity of human life

The emotional tone is reverent and assured. It affirms that life, identity, marriage, and purpose are not random; they are crafted by God's sovereign and loving hand.

Lord, My Defender

This poem is a worship declaration grounded in spiritual warfare and identity in Christ. It centers on dependence, protection, and readiness to stand firm through God's power. The imagery strongly reflects the Armor of God from Ephesians 6, but it is expressed personally and devotionally.

"Lord, You are my peace in the fiercest storm,
My strength, my refuge, my sheltered form."

The poem opens in trust. God is portrayed as stability amid chaos. The "storm" represents trials, emotional turmoil, or spiritual attacks. Instead of collapsing under pressure, the speaker finds covering and safety in Him.

"Your lamp lights the path where my feet now tread,
Ready to move where the Gospel is spread."

This echoes Psalm 119:105, God's Word guiding each step. The speaker is not just protected; she is commissioned. She walks with purpose, ready to advance the Gospel.

"Your helmet of salvation shields my mind,
protecting my thoughts, no longer bound."

The battle is first mental. Salvation protects the mind from fear, lies, doubt, and condemnation. "No longer bound" suggests previous mental captivity that has now been broken.

"No more will I conform to this world's design,
For Your truth renews this heart of mine."

This reflects Romans 12:2, transformation through renewal. The speaker rejects worldly standards and aligns her heart with divine truth.

*"You guard my soul with righteousness' might,
A breastplate strong, shining with light."*

The breastplate represents moral and spiritual protection. Righteousness guards the heart, the seat of identity and emotion. Light imagery suggests purity and clarity.

*"In You, O Lord, I stand firm.
In Your presence, forever secure."*

This is stability language. Standing firm implies resistance against attack. Security is not circumstantial; it is rooted in divine presence.

*"Your shield of faith blocks every lie.
Every curse that dares to fly."*

Faith becomes defense. Lies and curses symbolize accusations, spiritual attacks, and negative declarations. Faith intercepts them before they penetrate.

*"The belt of truth holds the armor tight.
Firmly, I stand, prepared to fight."*

Truth anchors everything. Without truth, the armor falls apart. The fight is spiritual, against deception, fear, and darkness.

*"Your Word, a living, breathing flame…
It separates joints, marrow, and bones,
It's sharper than any sword ever known."*

This references Hebrews 4:12. The Word is active, penetrating, discerning motives and thoughts. It is both a weapon and a purifier.

"My God is active, mighty to save.
My Defender, Protector, strong and brave."

God is not distant. He intervenes. He rescues. He fights on behalf of the believer.

"For in Your strength, I'm victorious till the end."

The poem closes in assurance. Victory is not self-achieved; it is sustained by God's strength. The endurance "till the end" reflects perseverance.

Overall, this poem explores:

• God as refuge in trials
• Spiritual armor and readiness
• Mental and emotional protection
• Renewal through truth
• Active spiritual warfare
• Confidence in divine victory

The tone is not fearful; it is fortified. The speaker does not deny the existence of battle but declares that she is fully equipped, fully covered, and ultimately victorious in Christ.

Healed of a Wicked Heart

This poem is a reflection on the condition of the human heart and the transforming power of God's Word. It weaves Scripture into testimony, moving from warning to redemption.

"It is not what enters the mouth that defiles
but what flows from within, what the tongue reveals."

The poem opens with Jesus' teaching that defilement is internal, not external. The focus is on the source of corruption, the heart. Words are presented as evidence of inner condition. Speech reveals what lives inside.

"For words spring forth from the depths of the heart,
piercing like arrows, tearing souls apart."

Here, words are described as weapons. They can wound deeply because they originate from the core of a person's being. This suggests accountability; harmful speech reflects unresolved internal issues.

"'The heart is deceitful, above all things,'
Its sickness is hidden, its motives unseen."

This echoes Jeremiah 17:9. The heart is not automatically trustworthy. It can conceal pride, bitterness, jealousy, or selfish ambition. The poem acknowledges that self-deception is real.

"Who can comprehend its secrets untold?
None but God, omnipotent, mighty, and strong."

Only God fully understands the human heart. This shifts the poem from human weakness to divine authority. God alone discerns hidden motives and intentions.

"Creator of worlds, Defender of grace.
Redeemer of souls, in His arms, we're safe."

The tone becomes worshipful. The God who judges the heart is also the One who protects and redeems it. Safety is found not in self-righteousness, but in His grace.

"His Word is the truth, sharp and divine.
It corrects, convicts, and fills hearts in time."

This references Hebrews 4:12, the Word as sharp and penetrating. Correction and conviction are not condemnation but refinement. The Word exposes sickness in order to heal it.

"Meditate daily, let His wisdom impart,
a life that is pure and blessed at heart."

Transformation requires discipline. Daily meditation on Scripture reshapes desires and thoughts. Purity begins internally.

"Those who endure to the end will prevail.
The last shall be first, their victory unveiled."

Perseverance becomes the path to victory. The poem affirms that faithfulness, not status, determines outcome in God's kingdom.

"I've run the race; the prize is mine,
For in His strength, I cross the finish line."

This is personal testimony. The author sees herself as enduring through struggle by God's strength, not her own ability.

Healed of a wicked heart. Jesus, He's Mine!"

The poem closes in redemption. The "wicked heart" has been transformed. Healing has occurred through a relationship with Christ. It ends not in fear of judgment, but in belonging.

Overall, this poem explores:

- The power of words as reflections of the heart
- The deceitful nature of the human heart
- God's omniscience and authority
- The refining power of Scripture
- The necessity of perseverance
- Personal transformation through Christ

The emotional arc moves from warning about internal corruption to celebration of internal healing. It is both cautionary and victorious, acknowledging the heart's danger while proclaiming that, in Jesus, it can be restored.

Show Your Truth, Lord

This poem is an intercessory cry wrapped in testimony. It speaks about spiritual blindness, human pride, and the contrast between worldly living and God's redemptive path. The tone is compassionate rather than condemnatory; the speaker pleads with others to see what she has come to know.

"Those who doubt will never understand your parables, or the mighty works of Your righteous hand."

The poem begins by addressing spiritual perception. Doubt here is not simple questioning; it suggests resistance and closed-heartedness. The parables symbolize deeper spiritual truths that require humility to grasp. Without openness, divine revelation remains hidden.

"They walk through life with their eyes tightly closed, hardened hearts, stiff necks…"

This language echoes biblical descriptions of stubbornness. "Hardened hearts" and "stiff necks" represent pride and unwillingness to submit. Regret grows because they refuse to release offense or bitterness.

"Unable to forgive, they carry the weight. of a world that crushes, sealing their fate."

Unforgiveness becomes a burden. The weight is self-imposed, carrying pain that God invites them to surrender. The world's system is portrayed as crushing and unforgiving.

"But Lord, I plead, help them see what is true.
Let them discover Your love that breaks through."

The tone shifts to prayer. The speaker is not attacking those who doubt; she intercedes for them. She believes revelation comes from God, not argument.

"Your way is the path of life and light.
While our way leads to heartache…"

Here, the poem contrasts divine will with human self-direction. God's way leads to peace and illumination; human pride leads to destruction. This is not a condemnation but a warning born from experience.

"You said Your yoke is lighter to bear
than the chains of this world…"

This references Jesus' promise that His burden is light. The "chains" symbolize sin, anxiety, worldly expectations, and pride. Surrender to God is portrayed as freedom, not restriction.

"You promised… to never depart,
to remain by our side and heal every heart."

This line centers on God's faithfulness. Unlike people who may abandon, God remains. Healing is relational; it comes through His presence.

"From my journey, I surely know your love."

Now the poem becomes a personal testimony. The speaker has experienced transformation firsthand. Her faith is not theoretical; it is lived.

"Your love, unfailing, covers sin's tide.
A shelter of grace where I now abide."

Sin once overwhelmed like a tide, but grace now shelters her. This suggests forgiveness and restoration.

"How could we turn from the One who redeems?
Who saves us from the enemy's schemes?"

This is rhetorical, expressing awe that anyone would reject redemption. The "enemy's schemes" represent spiritual deception and temptation.

"When we fall, Lord, You catch us in stride..."

This emphasizes mercy. Failure does not disqualify; God intervenes.

"Jesus, Jehovah, our Savior divine.
Forever and always, our hearts are Thine."

The poem ends in covenantal devotion. It moves from concern for the spiritually blind to reaffirming personal allegiance.

Overall, this poem explores:

• Spiritual blindness and pride
• The burden of unforgiveness
• Intercessory prayer for others
• The contrast between God's path and worldly living
• Personal testimony of transformation
• Devotion and covenant with Christ

The emotional arc moves from lament over hardened hearts to celebration of divine faithfulness. It reads like someone who has tasted grace and now longs for others to experience the same light.

Author Bio

Ebony Brinson is a multi-genre author, poet, and creative entrepreneur whose words are rooted in faith, healing, and transformation. Born and raised in the Bronx, New York, Ebony writes from lived experience, allowing her work to speak honestly about brokenness, redemption, and the unwavering grace of God.

Her poetry collection, *Illumination Through Darkness: Poetry That Pours from the Soul,* is a deeply personal reflection of her spiritual journey. Through raw and heartfelt verses, Ebony explores themes of betrayal, heartbreak, faith, surrender, and divine restoration. Her writing reveals that even in life's darkest moments, the light of God's love can heal, restore, and transform the human heart.

As the founder of **Woman of Many Trades**, Ebony is passionate about helping others discover the power of their voice through writing, publishing, and creative expression. She works closely with aspiring authors and entrepreneurs, guiding them from idea to publication while encouraging them to share their stories with courage and authenticity.

Ebony's mission is simple but powerful: to remind others that pain does not have the final word. Through faith, resilience, and obedience to God's calling, darkness can become the very place where light begins to shine. Through her words, Ebony invites readers into a journey of healing, spiritual reflection, and renewed hope.

Publisher's Note:
From Woman of Many Trades

"Every powerful book begins with one thing: an idea."

An idea that won't let you sleep. An idea that keeps whispering, *"Tell it."* At **Woman of Many Trades**, we believe your story deserves to be told with boldness, clarity, and confidence. Your voice is not ordinary; it's impactful. It's generational. It has the power to shift perspectives, heal hearts, spark conversations, and leave a legacy long after the last page is turned. We don't just publish books. We build authors.

From the very first brainstorm to the final printed copy in your hands, we walk with you every step of the journey. Whether you're outlining and planning your manuscript, structuring your chapters, refining your message, formatting your interior, or perfecting grammar and flow, we ensure your book is polished, professional, and positioned for success.

We also assign you your own unique ISBN number for all desired formats of your book, allowing it to be distributed and sold worldwide. Your work is properly registered, professionally presented, and prepared to stand confidently in the global marketplace. This isn't just about words on paper. This is about ownership. This is about authority. This is about building something that outlives you. It's about turning your lived experiences, your expertise, your creativity, and your voice into a tangible legacy, something that can sit on shelves across the world and in the hands of readers who need exactly what you carry.

At Woman of Many Trades, we transform ideas into finished works of excellence and aspiring writers into confident, positioned, published authors. Your story matters. Your voice matters. And the world is waiting. Let's build it together.

www.womanofmanytrades.com
Woman of Many Trades LLC
CEO & Founder Ebony Brinson